LAVENDER

BY

CHRISTOPHER POINDEXTER

Cover Art by Jeremy Brown
Instagram: @artistjeremybrown
theartofjeremybrown.com

Monarch Publishing, 2017
www.monarchbookstore.com

I would like to dedicate this book to a young Italian woman named Clara, who birthed my love for poetry when I was eighteen. The moment you handed me *The Picture of Dorian Grey* was the moment I began to find poetry in absolutely everything.

LAVENDER

TONIGHT

GEORGE RAFT

STOLEN HARMONY

BEN BERNIE

STAN LAUREL
OLIVER HARDY

ATION PHOTOGRAPHS

New Orle

I will never forget
my first love.
the way she spoke,
laughed, loved,
existed,
and I find myself
thinking of her often,
remembering what it was like
to be spilled into her arms.
I think of her dancing
somewhere in the streets
of Italy,
giddy with wine
in her belly.
If I could tell her
one thing right now,
it would how incredibly
thankful I am for her love
when it was with me,
how much it has made me
the man I am today,
and how because of her
and only her,
I have found a lover
in poetry.
thy love.
thy dearest.

often it is the most simple things
that root me into the earth,
reminding me that my body
is a magic thing,
a world wonder

so I cling to these things,
full moon, bohemian kisses, sunsets
and reading books by mother ocean

as if they were the only thing
that could save me,
and save me,
they do.

I am searching
for things and people
that will mold me
like some shapeshifter
into the artist I long to be,
say it be a certain tune
or book
or poem
or woman.
I live on bent knees
towards these things,
offering my open
eccentric heart
as an invitation,
"step inside
and bring with you
your light,"
my mentors,
my muses,
my darling
beloved teachers.

isn't it an absolute magical thing
how magnificent and grand
and diverse this world is,
yet we can meet our significant
other in a coffee shop
or bookstore or bar?
how incredibly lovely is this?
Doesn't it just make you want
to get up each faithful morning,
put on your favorite attire,
spine the fitting jazz record,
and walk out of your door
with the exquisite hope
that your love
may be waiting for you
through some glass window
reading some book
dreaming of romance
and the color lavender
and the sacred skin
of some other?

we wait for this our entire lives.
what a day to be alive.

"Rocking Chair"

We cannot be whole by simply
wishing we were whole.
We cannot taste greatness
on our lips that way,
either.
So above all,
my beautiful, peculiar,
translucent child–
be passionate.
It matters not what you're
passionate about,
only that you are.

FRENCH
AND
ITALIAN BREAD

ROLLS
AND
DOUGHNUTS

6173 m

Longshoremen's strike, New Orleans 1935 Photo by Shahn 23...

N.Y.P.
PICTURE COLL...

They all line up
in this house I worship,
mosaic tiles, chandeliers
and enchanting oval mirrors,
the everyday stranger,
the homeless,
the widows,
the patients,
the madmen,
the vulnerable.
I search for their essence,
their purity
in all of the glistening
shadows of light,
and I am reminded of something,
something that always desires me,
always consumes me,
it arrives like a winded whisper
soft enough to declare
you alive;

Today is the day of love.

As it, has always been.

11, 1935

You will find
in due time
the things
you spend your days
worrying about
never really mattered
at all.

Flesh is just flesh and bones are just bones,

I look you in the eyes
and know
a home
is only as beautiful
as its windows.

how many skins do you wear?
how many times do you allow yourself to shed?
these are questions I get when I think too much over
too much afternoon wine in a bedroom alone,
staring out the window
as an older lady walks her dog
and a big bald man walks across his lawn for the paper
and in some other country a little child
starves to death
while another country gets richer and richer
and our eyes get smaller and smaller
and smaller.

oh oh may I ask you again
how many skins
have you lived in?
and how many times do you allow yourself to shed?

how many lives have you led?

listen and listen close with the
only soul that you know-
only with a thousand eyes will we ever
see it all.

People tell me too often
to just accept the blessings
that come my way-
the money, the shelter,
life without struggle.
They tell me I think too much.
I say
"tell me why the hell should
I be so comfortable,
while others are
so poor, so lacking,
so horrified? tell me?"

They say it is none of my business.
That I should not worry about those
I do not know.
And I hate that. I despise it.
I believe we all are in this together,
every day, every bleeding second.
When one human suffers, we all suffer.
But fuck, who am I but just
a sensitive little boy
with a hurricane of love
inside him too strong and foolish
for his own good.

My sensitivity is a curse.
I will always understand that.
But I would still rather be this way
than be like them.
Forgetting the ones we are not
"responsible" for sounds like the worst
kind of silent inner torture.

you can't
have too much
of anything or
you will ruin
it.

if you want to
keep things
beautiful and poignant
you must find the time
to miss them.

at the end of the day,
all I care for is purpose.
sweet purpose.
I think back to the feeling of watering plants,
taking the dogs for a walk,
working on that first buzz
as the birds chirp sweetly
through the morning,
kissing my woman before she leaves for work,
writing something down that kills the exhaustion
in me and maybe if I am lucky,
a few others.
my days are very simple.
nothing special,
but it scratches away at me to find meaning
in even the tiniest of things,
and often, I do.
honestly, this is my only salvation.

I rest easy when the world is full of small,
strange color.

Fear
when we look in the mirror,
fear
when we look at others,
fear
when we look at the world,
fear
when we look at our dreams
and think they exist somewhere
our eager toes will not
allow us to go.

I don't have a problem with
us being afraid,
I have a problem with
us being afraid
of the wrong things.

I have never been too sure of anything.
I see too many walls, too much
hesitation, too many false idol eyes.
I gaze at the night sometimes and
even the stars appear as hypocrites.
I have no idea who to believe, what to
be, what to perceive, where to plant
my veins in the bottomless soil.
This leaves me quiet, alone in the mind,
misinterpreted by those who chase
the daze of translucent thunder.

I walk underneath everyone,
hurricane-eyed and awaken.

Always in the shadow of the willow
and that is why it is weeping.

-Christopher Poindexter and Lei Jenelle

Man can find himself locked away
in many prisons.
Some visible, some only in the mind.
That same man has the key
to get out of them,
but not always the awareness and strength.
I pray to whatever God there is-
man, nature, heaven, cosmos-
grant me that strength.
Grant me the ability to always rise triumphant
above the thick darkness.

There will always be more light than we know.
Always more, never less.

May we always yearn to find it.

grandfather taught me that words are bullets
they are not soft feathers
they are not delicate flowers
we have them to punch our enemies in the skulls
and this is the way his tongue flowed
war still a thought kept in his t-shirt pocket
humor his only way to drown
the gunfire in Vietnam
they say you are what you do
you are what you experience
and to the core of a person this rings true
boy does it
he left this earth yelling at and punching
the people who love him most
but he was ill, he had been for a long time
and his mind was somewhere else
and we all knew that
but it made it that much more difficult
to say goodbye to a man
pegged as an asshole
but who beneath it all
had a heart as soft
as a mother's love for her infant
as delicate as that very infant's
cold hands wrapped divinely
around her mother's
thumb.

my only hope now is that I love you the way
they loved each other. every one that knew
them proclaimed it was like watching a romantic
film. I can see their first greeting now-
grandpa gathered around a flock of women,
buying them all shots, grandma watching from
a corner, drinking tequila putting all the men
around her under the table. he must have seen
her spirit right there in the moment, I imagine
it as clear as day, 15 shots to kill the pain,
but never enough to take away her sweetness.
she was nothing less than an angel.
he was nothing more than human.
I think what kept them going is they always
knew how to meet in the middle.

New Orleans, La. 1935. 6214 M-1. Photo by Shahn. 23

As the morning birds sing my burdens for me
I limp to the fountain of my youth
wanting nothing more than to feel
the smile that once hung from my face
like a diamond chandelier.
Grandpa used to put that there.

Now I must ask myself the question,
"who the hell will do that now?"
certain people shape our lives in certain ways,
and when you lose them,
you are left with a black hole their ghost
can't quite replace.

I grab his old hat grandma gave me,
smell the top of it,
goddammit that English leather scent
does the trick every time.

Nothing brings to life
again
a warm memory like
fragrance.

MAE BUSCH and CHARLEY HALL
Directed by CHARLES LOCALS
A Metro-Goldwyn-Mayer PICTURE

I am always looking for something.
up, down, around and through
my eyes find themselves begging for the
next thing to sail them away.
Nothing is ever satisfied in this
body of mine.
Should I take this pill to feel
the world or should I leave it alone
and feel the bare and bruised nothing?
You tell me delicate one
tell me what you have been through
and what makes you do what
you do?
Tell me of fallen friends and lovers
of wild air and burning hope
tell me of your dark
and how the moon likes to curl
up to it every single night
without warning.
Tell me how you want to be better and why
your hands will not let you.
I want to know it all.
When everyone is afraid to speak
the truth,
I dare you to.

McLACHLEN BANKING CORPORATION

FORTIS ET FIDUS

UNDER SUPERVISION OF U.S. TREASURY

PHOTO
SOURCE #11.1937.

If only
our bodies
would marry
the beauty
growing inside
them, it wouldn't
be so
exhausting trying
to love
ourselves.

I do not understand why she is this way,
blind to the whimsical truth that is her and
her alone.
She is a type of soft magic that I have
not seen any other human be.
I have heard her weep like the rivers do
and the desert longs to- always wanting what
she does not own.
She clasps her hands together but
the truth slips through her quivering fingers;

I want her to love what I love,
something beyond body, beyond words,
beyond soul even.

I want her to love herself so deeply that
she is carried away to some warm fantasy

and I want her to return to me
tasting of only mother nature

and I will strip her down
and make love to her

naked with lilacs
and orange moons and
the abundance of forgotten
stars.

nema. New Orleans, La. 1935. 6214 M-3. Photo by Shahn. 2390

We know
so perfectly
how to give birth
to the monsters
inside us,
but for reasons I
will never figure out,
we have not the slightest
clue of what to do
with all the
love.

Not only did I love her,
but I could tell the universe
loved her, too.
More than others.
She was different.
after all,
I would be a fool
not to notice the way
the sunshine played
with her hair.

Steel Chapel

Felicity Road New Orleans   J.W.W.

the light I see you in will never fade,
it will move, sway like winds and waves,
but it will always carry the same name.
love is love love is torture
love is strength love is foolish
love is fame
love is poor love is proud
love is weak love is flowers
love is death
love is life
love is a mausoleum
of bodies alive
love is all we have
all we have is
this

I'll kiss you in places
you have never been
kissed

love, is endless.

MARDI GRAS
FEBRUARY 12TH
1907

The night was cold as it always is,
your lips wet with cosmic desire.
I saw you where you stood,
wherever it was,
whatever name you had for it.

I can say there are many reasons why a man loves a woman.
But, when the eye forfeits reason, when it looks past the
vision and energy of the world and blissfully stares straight
into the soul, reasons die. They are no longer needed.

And goodness do I feel that way tonight. You and I,
white with heaven.

I always loved the way you looked in that dress.
I try to find a word for it but divinity like this is nameless.

My sweet and only,
I want to cover you,
cover you in whichever way
you desire to be covered.
With orchards and emeralds and
intimacy like wind kissing
the pockets of earth.
I want the beauty to be
overwhelming.
I want it to seep into your skin.

I want to love you into oblivion
and I want you to tremble
when you feel it.

hello my little gentle soul of effort,
come back to me now,
like a child.
there are a thousand paths
you can go
but they all must not
be so.
choose what you must,
what stirs in you
like blood and love,
like only something
true.
hello my little gentle soul of effort,
why don't you just choose you?

The thing is, I can see you when
I am not even looking.

The universe is a carpenter constructing love in the
eyes of those who are brave enough
to believe in it.

This morning I told you,

"I used to throw the word forever around
like a leather-laced ball in the summer.
As if it was a game of routine.
I have shed my boyish skin since then.
Now I dream of you and I
teaching each other to count
on four hands to infinity."

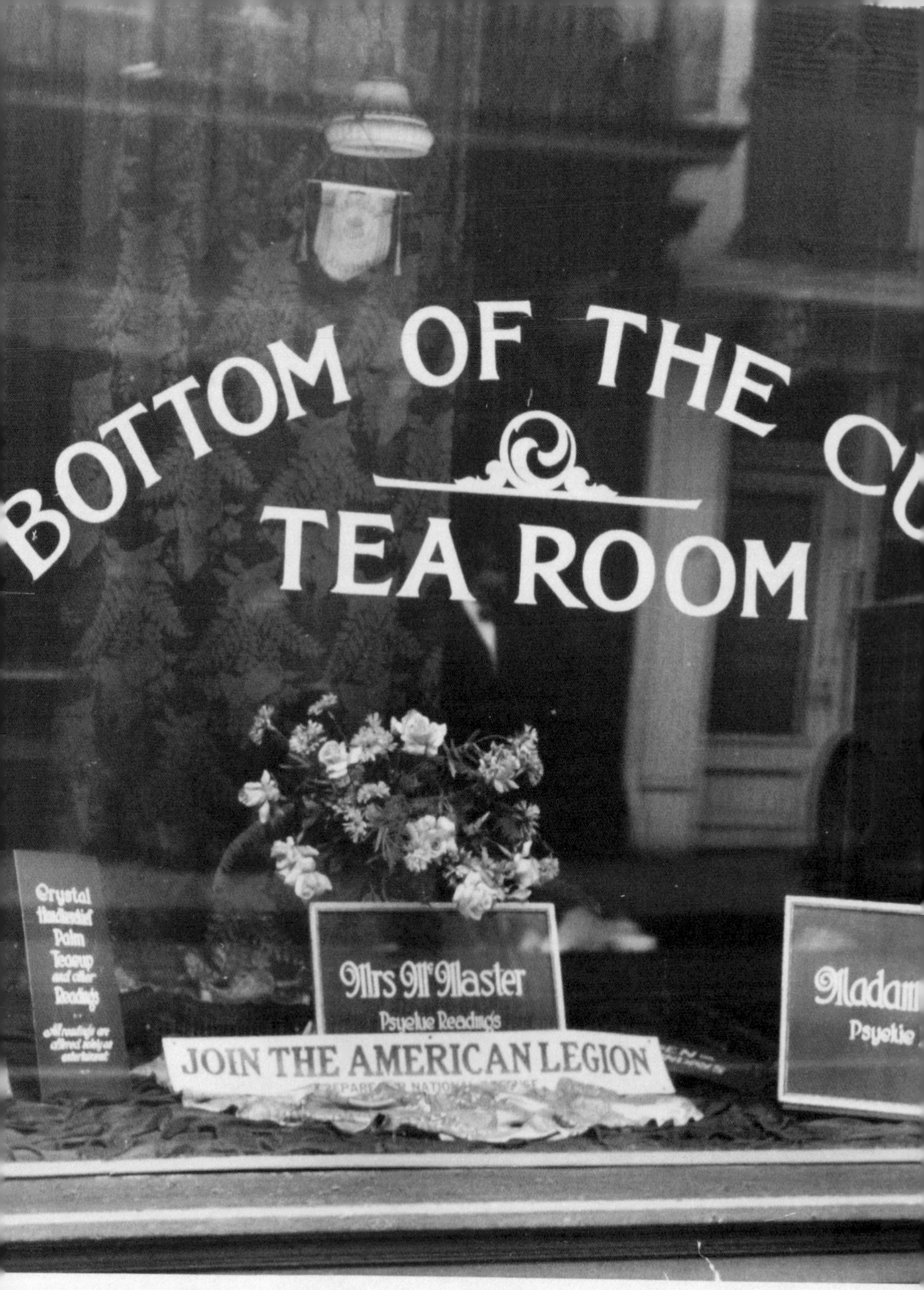

PHOTO SOURCE 11.1941.

Her dress slides down her curious legs;
outside the window,
a bird chants a prophecy that arouses
the damp ground.
Her dress hits the floor, stunned.
I, too;
nature and her trembling inside me
all at once.

New Orleans, La. 1935.
Jackson Square. The

the day wants your eyes, the pebbled ground longs for your feet,
awake my sweet, how magnificent is this naked morning.
when I say I have loved you all this time
you mustn't doubt me.
your eyes are my eyes, your hands my hands,
touch what I fear and I am no longer afraid.
they say a woman can save a man, bring him to a land
he does not know, and I concur. the seas here glisten more
the moons beg better questions and the answers come more gently and
are less tiresome. it is amazing what a woman can do to a man.
amazing the ways she can sculpt him. without you I am less,
I say with a hand lightly draped over my chest. oaths are forever.
this love is like waters returned to stone, like birds resting-
atop wavering trees, like moons sunk in the emerald ocean,
nature sings to us and through us and because of us. without us
it is without love. without love it is nothing. when we go
to sleep the world sleeps.

the eyes of a little boy tired and alone prepare to close as we
turn out the lights,
one last kiss until the waiting morning.

have you ever experienced something
so astonishingly beautiful,
you wanted nothing more
than for that moment to be burned
and in your mind be born
fresh once more?

the greatest second you will
ever have on this earth is
the exact moment you fell
in love.

Still hazel and cloudy. North East wind, cold & damp. Tendency to rain in the afternoon and a rain after night fall —

Studied the principles of Gothic Vaulting and the equilibration of arches after an early tea —

Cold north wind. to North west. quite brisk — clear & sunshine & mild and sunny in the afternoon

Answered Mr. C. Gillett's letter of 22nd inst.

Recent arrivals confirm the report of the Czar's death and the accession of his son Alexander

Marble cutting at the   J. M. 18

Do you believe, too, like I do,
that all of our bodies are connected,
even if in the tiniest way? How beautiful
could that be, my love? That we carry
pieces of each other inside us?

the day we met, we knew-
we were kindred souls.
people like us
only came around once
every blue moon
and I could not tell you
enough
how dazzling it was
to know that for that night
the universe wore
a dress
the color of indigo.

I think a part of my sadness stems from the notion
that I do not carry a vocabulary magnificent enough to
set your true brilliance into motion.

They ask me what the chandelier upon the ceiling looks like
when I dance upon the floor inside of you and I will not tell them.
Why the hell would I? In my jealous mind you are all mine.
But I will say any man who looks at you and doesn't fall in love
instantly is a fool. You are the kind of person a stranger
stands by and immediately feels more loved. Your presence
makes life more bearable for anyone you are around.
You have told me your eyes swell up and your heart nearly
bursts into a thousand pieces because you have no clue
what you are doing in life and what your gift is,
but hear me out darling, accept these words,
I bow these hands and letters on knees of their own-
your gift is love. The energy of it. All of it.
You soak in every damn thing you touch. You make it warm.
Soothed. Tell me, how is that not a gift?
And when are you going to accept it?

when you kiss me
lights go off
on the edge of
the world.
when you kiss me
children rise
from their beds and begin
their day in perfect
innocence.
when you kiss me the clouds shift
and comfort the hurting
and they never seem to
hurt again.
when you kiss me
all of our heroes are summoned from
the dead and
come to live inside
our chests.
when you kiss me I am as good
as I will ever get,
as pure as you will ever know me,
as perfect as your eyes will allow me,
so hear me when I say
darling,
when you kiss me,
I become
a better man.

I think
you feel so much
because you kiss the world
silently
with the soul of your eyes
and never ask for
a reply.

THE
NEW ST. CHARLES
NEW ORLEANS

MARDI GRAS

February 12th
1907

Imagine a world in black and white.
Everything. Our feelings are named different names.
Our art becomes different things.
I walk my dogs and see black
and white houses, black and white lawns,
black and white dreams
coming from windows where little children
wait patiently to be removed from
their deep sleep.
Imagine the first moment of color,
but imagine it in this way-
you never know of anything
but black and white until you
fall in love, and then
she comes to you,
like never before, stumbling
drunk through the front door,
a hand full of purple and
blue and red and yellow,
it is an offering,
a surrender,
"here,
have my heart,
have my color."

Coliseum Place
New Orleans

I don't think they understand, perhaps even I don't
just yet- I need you so that I can be what I cannot be
on my own. Inside me is something ancient wounds
have made me. I am scarred beneath the skin of my skin.
But you know this. Do you remember that day you asked
for my soul and in return I spit out gravel? It is no
different now. My hands are still tragedies, tying a noose
around the neck of anything they try too long to hold.
But you, you have always had this way about you, this way
that is in my grandmother and my mother and every decent
human being on this earth- you see the best in people,
always, no matter what the cost. Tell us, how can that
be done? Grant me your telescope eyes for the moment.
I want to see what only the speed of light has time for.

as the day flourishes in its routine,
the earth stands passionate
in its baby blue coat,
wondering when we
who
from above
look like tiny ants
parading against each other,

will stop the unnecessary war.

love is the answer, the sun weeps,
again and again and again,
as the fiery-eyed moon braces itself
for pathetic, blooming
chaos.

I watch the dark green candle burn in its thick glass
as I try to fall asleep but sleep will not grant
me its reward.
Sometimes I think I love you too much.
You stand tall above my world in slow motion
Playing the part of a mountain that changes its
shape every time my heart shakes.
At night I dream we walk together in forests
of evergreen and
climb trees pretending to be things
only a child's eye can manifest.

Don't you see, my sweet baby?
It has always been you.
There is no one else.

Will you walk with me
hand in hand
on days
when the rain feels like soft bullets pressed
to my porcelain skin?

Will you be my temporary end?

For death will be a pause we maintain
until
we grow bold and in love
spiraling like smiling infants
into a brand new
breathtaking
world.

Yesterday we had the best sex we have had in years.
Birds sang outside our windows like they knew
our troubles by name and gender
and maybe their song was a way to begin
a spiritual revolution.
Inside us wept a thousand new lives scratching
to get out.
Who had we become?
And who did we truly want to be?

"I think I will be mountain. I think I will be purple.
I think I will be the stillness of energy."

"I think I will be sea. I think I will be yellow.
I think I will be free."

The sweat dripped from our backs
onto the bed
in the shape of the people we once were

and we haven't seen them since.

leans from the

I am in love with her because she is the
only woman to ever understand me to
the bone and even further.

And there is nothing more beautiful
than the arousing of a place
no one has ever touched.

LYDIA THOMPSON.

Mora

707 BROADWAY, N.Y.

strolling through the heart
of Los Angeles
the whole world shows up
in all sorts of different garments-
men in suits,
men without suits,
street performers,
architects,
tourists,
prostitutes,
all of them, in their daily routine,
their daily inevitable fight.
there is more life in some of
them than the others,
more fire,
but the truth for the majority
of them at least,
remains the same,
never swaying, never changing,
always, this-
no one wants to love
but everyone wants to
get paid.

the system has made us this way.

The people will tell you not to be too gentle,
but you must steer your tired ears in different
directions. Tilt your neck to all that is hard to
see and listen to the trees to the waters to the
birds to the silent song the earth plays when
one human being falls in love with another,
I swear I have seen the sun shake in the morning.
I have slept in the imaginary cardboard boxes
of the mind I have drank myself lifeless before
the sun reaches the top of the sky
I have seen my grandmother clutch my dying
grandfather's body for days at a time, married
around him until the last breath left his exhausted
lungs. I have seen death and I have wanted to die
I have seen poverty and murder in the eyes of men
I have seen the homeless sleep silently on the
sidewalk with their dogs next to them and the
people just go by and by and by thankful to not
be that hungry but too foolish to see the human
spirit in the weakened. I say that I have seen it
all and say it with a sure tongue to say this-
there is no such thing as too gentle. Too kind.
Too loving. This world makes people hard, and there
is an understanding there, one we must learn,
but we can't let those people decide for us. The
world is as kind and soft as you see it. As you
let it be. Love is not for the weak, and those
who have told you that know it, they are just too
fucking terrified to admit it. Because love is the
most painful sting there is. But just as
it takes away it gives a thousand times more.

So return to the throne, right here in the chest
of the world, the sun rises and sets in the east
and the west and in-between love spills out from
the middle.

Limberg en Stirie.
...es et gravées d'après nature par Thérèse de Hollein 1813.

I never thought I would settle down with a woman.
My father taught me there are too many pearls
at the bottom of the sea to take the risk
of swimming up with just one.
He said, "fill your pockets while you can son."

Do you remember the day we first made love?
I didn't know how much I loved you then,
I knew I did, but I wasn't aware of the intensity.
I had no clue one day I would wear your
spirit on my body like a blanket to keep me
warm.

Do you know how fucking terrifying it is to look
someone in the eye and say
the words, "I couldn't live without you."?

I swore I would never be here.
I swore and I meant it.

I have never been more happy to call
my own bluff.

the sun complicates the moon
while
the sky complicates the soil
while
the hand complicates the pen
while
the soul complicates the heart
while
the father complicates the child
while
life complicates death
while
all things complicate things
that were never meant to be complicated
while
we run our minds on never-ending
tracks of worry and confusion
while
the earth just waits for us,
whispering to itself
as
its head tilts
towards the edge of
fantastic oblivion,

"it all could be much simpler,
if only they would focus
on their becoming."

sometimes
I brush my sadness
off like four fingertips
to a feather
on the edge
of my shoulder

and just watch
it float there in the wind

interpreting it like
a dream
that has a thousand
different meanings.

I have learned to let the wind speak to me.
I drive around on my bike with sunglasses on and a
drink
in hand and feel the sun splash against my needy
face.
It shows the child in me its birth.
I see mothers and fathers walking their dogs and
children riding their skateboards and bikes and in
these
tiny moments they all
appear as gods. All their lives are extraordinary.
Filled with such color.
I smile and they smile back, and somehow, it's
majestic.
I find this grand wavering nostalgia in other people.
As if I knew them in another life.
Every time I look at a stranger I feel attached to
them.
And when they walk away, it breaks my goddamn
heart.

I never knew her name
but she always walked my street
And I would glance at her through
my desk window
and I just loved her for
her consistency, commitment.
She was always on time;
every morning around nine a.m.
I would make a cup of coffee and
sit down and smoke and there
she was- long legs, in her forties
maybe, beautiful long brown hair.
She intrigued me so much because
she was something different, mysterious,
new, and
she gave me ten seconds of her life
everyday,
I never needed to ask for it.
I wanted to know her life, her wounds,
her children's names, what keeps her up
at night, her lost dreams and found ones,
and what she thinks of death.
I wanted to know it all.
But carefully. I wanted her to tell
it to me each time she walked by that window,
just as I liked to think she did,
with movements, with mystery, with my
grand wandering imagination.
I wanted to create her in a way
that made it impossible for her to
walk away.

My three dogs watch me from the window
as I sit on the balcony with blank eyes
going to war with a blank page as if the world
was not plentiful with grace and yellow-spirited
absolution. Their eyes are the grace. All six of them.
Jazz soft pedals in the background as they sleep,
dream and wake at the faint sound of my woman's
feet whispering across the oak floor. I don't think
I love anything more than I love dogs. Without
pause and reward they love everything around them
with an intensity foreign to my childless eyes.
I want people to be aware of that intensity. To keep
it close. To know when they see these gentle
creatures being walked down the street that there is
most certainly little gods among them. Love among
them. Peace. Hope. Grace as pure as the rising sun.

Flow, such a better thing than force,
words fall like waterfalls off the breasts
of soulful women, we watch them
make rivers men
are too afraid and stupid to swim in.
What would be your name if you
named yourself?
I would call myself courage
so that maybe if someone said my name enough
I might actually grow the guts to
leap for freedom.
Flow, such a better thing than force,
love bores lust while lust looks for
new flesh to live in
prowling earth like a jungle cat
stubborn and eager for her
next prey.

The wild things love to be fucked
the gentle things love to slow dance.

Either way legs get tired
and we all carry the same fear inside us-

in the end we may go out alone.

My eyes force themselves open
and from the smoke
my hands appear;
flawed, purple,
I am not the man I thought I was.
Are we ever?
Even the most pure beings
wear their plastic masks around
like Halloween children
smiling at the death of day.

I just don't want to stare at my true self
when I die and say,
"you are the one that got away."

I must build a space
where creativity is abundant,
where it does not deny me,
where it flows
like soft waters
through rocks that do not
question their purpose,
something as simple
as a child's golden eye
as he first learns to tie
his shoe,
yet as complex as the
center of the soul
where the true human exists
in everyone
too frightened to come out
but too bold and full
to burn away and die.

What to say that hasn't been said
already?
With what intensity shall I love?
We spend our days mocking
those before us,
and I have failed collecting
the words that describe you.
The words that will tell your taste,
your touch.
Why must they deny me?

I suppose some things are just
that dazzling,
just that beauteous.

I take one look at you and
my mouth drips with silence.

"keep being sensitive,"
the mountains tell me.
the flowers.
the drink.
the stranger.
the music.
"keep being sensitive,"
life screams.
delicacy is
a forgotten art.

we stand in front of mirrors
hoping they will say something
lovely back
but they only have filthy tongues
and tell us
what we do not have.

we know the secrets of the world, the secrets
that sit like great big chests at the foot of
our mothers' beds. we know them but we do not
understand them. we hear them but do not listen.
we move but our souls do not move with us.
we know the secrets of the world, but we ignore them;
a newly crowned widow walking up the stairs of a
catholic church, dreaming of a body that once stood
ruby-eyed next to her. in this moment she is the
portrait of love- it ends like a train crashing into
the stone hand of god.
we know the secrets of the world, but we disown them;
two men sitting together on a bench in new orleans,
drinking coffee and kissing as the sun weeps and
slivers through the buildings. the stares they get are
ancient. something that should have been buried
long ago, or not born at all.
we know the secrets of the world, but we change them;
fourteen men in black suits sit at a round table
overlooking New York City, what we do not know is
they have us all by the balls. they move us like
puppets and we strut like we are our own creators.
how blind is our own blindness.
we know the secrets of the world, but we don't
appreciate them; an old homeless soldier sits on the
corner of a city block, his sign reads, "she had a
better lawyer." he could be full of shit but
who isn't? love still drips from his brow and falls
into his eyes but we just tell ourselves we do not
have the time. we do not have the time.
we know the secrets of the world, we carry them,
we feel them, we are them. we dance upon a crystal
floor where the possibilities are endless.
we are everything and nothing all at once.

and we do have a choice.

Where are your eyes?
Where are your eyes while
little girls with hearts of giants
lose their soul on crowded streets
to big men with hearts of stone?
Where are your eyes?
Where are your eyes while
a village of children slip into
a coma of sadness
their bellies carved by inevitable
blindness and starvation?
Where are your eyes?
Where are your eyes while
the animals of the world bearing
more soul than humans
get trampled by the humans themselves
and left for dead in circuses and
careless zoos sucking money
through a silver tube?
Where are your eyes I ask and
ask again as the world spins
on an axis of mental slavery and
invisible disease
I want to know where are they
those big, ancestor eyes
where are they when all the love
in the world is sleeping
sleeping in your bones
in their bones
in the marvelous soul of
the forbidden soil.

Since I was young I knew I wasn't like the other men.
I didn't walk the way they did, I didn't talk the way they did,
I didn't dress the way they did. I never wanted to.
The ego-driven ones made me sick the most,
though I knew they had their own suffering,
and their swelling heads were just a cover up
for how soft they truly were.
I saw the masks from an early age, called everyone's bluff,
even my own, and this is why I choose sensitivity. Vulnerability.
Still knowing so many of the women do not long for it.
They want a man with strong shoulders, one with swift confidence.
They want electric faces and sharp rib-cages, deep pockets
and fierce red knuckles, none of which I have.
But I still love the women. There is nothing I appreciate more.
Everyday I think of all the ones I have loved, could love,
will never love, nearly loved.
I am staring at one now in this bar in the airport,
she is in her thirties perhaps, divine, long blonde hair,
glasses, a tan winter coat, drinking red wine.
When she walks away a part of me will diminish,
grow old as if I have loved her for decades,
the bar doors, her deathbed.
This is just how I am. I think too much. I feel too much.
My vulnerability, always, infinitely present.
I would try to change it, but I have no desire to.
I don't want to be like the other men.
Wearing their grit like a ribbon just to dazzle the women.
I don't believe them. Not for one second.

And it's okay, because they don't believe me,
either.

what to make of this beautiful elderly Asian man
slouched awkwardly over,
feeding food to a squirrel that does tricks
for him, spins and backflips,
as if the man is here every single day with persistence,
at central park,
showing love and affection to this same creature,
how does the squirrel always know when to show?
does he know more than we know?
there is more love and pureness in this
than anything.
the man,
more wise and brave
than our politicians,
our school systems,
our egos,
our churches.

the squirrel, too.

I'm building a house for my woman,
but you mustn't tell her,
it's a secret.
The windows will be made from
the color of her eyes.
I hope to see the world through her.
The walls will consist of the most
ancient stones,
our home filled with the spirit of
old souls.
The scent inside will reminisce
our loved ones,
so that we will never feel as if we
are without love.
This home will be perfect,
It will be pure.
The chandeliers will glisten when our
minds are dark with death.
The stairs will applaud our willingness
to rise.
The rooms will haunt our frenzied emotions.
The water will come from the tears of
complete strangers and wash us new.
This home will be perfect,
it will be pure;

The days of her not finding the strength
to love herself will be no more.

CHRISTOPHER MARK POINDEXTER
is currently traveling the U.S. with a typewriter collecting stories.

instagram: @christopherpoindexter
twitter: @ChristopherPoin
christopherpoindexter.org